# CONTENTS

# WELCOME TO MINECRAFT

**Minecraft is home to adventure, action and creativity. It's a world of heroes, monsters and battles.**

**W**elcome to Minecraft. Whether you are a new adventurer, or have been wandering the biomes for years, Minecraft is a perfect place to call home.

Even if you've never played Minecraft, it's likely you know about it. Minecraft is the bestselling video game of all-time. It has sold over 238 million copies - that's more copies than there are people in the country of Brazil!

Minecraft is the most watched video game on YouTube, and there are more videos made about Minecraft than any other game. It's a worldwide phenomenon that has captured the hearts of players young and old, and after 12 years, there is no sign of stopping.

The game can be played in several ways; using your creativity to build fantastic buildings or sculptures; or as an adventure where you build your world, equip yourself with weapons and armour, and venture to fight the Ender Dragon.

**T**he world is filled with unique opportunities, exciting items, friendly and enemy creatures to live with or battle against. The only thing you need is some courage, as well as some imagination.

Grab your sword, pack some food, and get ready for the best adventure you've ever experienced.

Minecraft can be played almost everywhere, including Xbox, PlayStation, Nintendo Switch, PC and Mobile.

**TIP!**

You can choose a level of difficulty for your survival world. If it's your first adventure, try it on easy - you can change it later if needed.

# PLAYING SURVIVAL

**Survival is the game mode most players will choose first, as it lays out a simple adventure in front of you. In Survival, you're not just mining and building, but also fighting monsters and exploring the world.**

There is only a loose guide to Survival - you spawn into the world, harvest materials, build structures and items, while moving towards the goal of defeating the Ender Dragon. Not all players who enjoy Survival Mode will even fight the dragon. While a set of people will constantly create new worlds in order to fulfil the life of an adventurer and end it all with the dragon fight.

There's so much to do in Minecraft, that it could take you hundreds of hours before even attempting that end fight. The thing to remember is that, in Survival Mode your character's life could end at any moment.

You have to master fighting mobs so you can harvest their materials, or gain experience points for enchanting items. Players need to monitor their hunger so that they don't starve. You can't fall from great heights; or stay underwater for too long; or stray too far from home without ending up lost.

The thing to remember is that everything is limited, you can run out of items and find yourself in danger.

# BEING CREATIVE

Whereas, in Creative Mode, there is no limit to the things you can do or the items you can use. The only limit is your imagination. Creative Mode is for those who want to build whatever is in their mind, with no restriction.

Have you ever wanted to build a football stadium in Minecraft? What about a rollercoaster? Or a zoo? You can construct any of these things and so many more because in your inventory sits every single item and material. Plus, you can use as much of it as you want.

This is your time to shine. Grab materials only found in the End and bring them to the Overworld; visit the Nether and create a villain's castle rising out of the lava.

If building isn't your thing, you can still use Creative Mode. You can simply explore if you l ike to see each of the biomes - grab an elytra and some fireworks and fly across the world. Seek out the things you've never seen before, or spawn in thousands of enemies just to see what would happen.

Let loose, have fun and don't let anything hold you back.

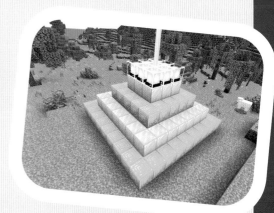

## TIP!

You don't have to build using Creative Mode, you can use it to simply fly around the world and find cool places. Or set hide and seek challenges for your friends.

# OVERWORLD BIOMES

The various biomes of Minecraft offer different things, depending on what you want from the game. Some are perfect for starting out an adventure, while others are great for supplying materials. Of course, there are a few biomes that are utterly empty, but gorgeous to visit. Whatever you need, there's a biome for you.

## EASIEST START - PLAINS

If you want the least challenging start in Minecraft, then the plains are for you. This biome is usually pretty flat, making building a starting base nice and simple, plus you can see all around you so that mobs can't creep up on you.

This biome also offers a lot of friendly animals that can be farmed, offering materials and food. The plains is one of only a few biomes where you will find villages that are great for trading (or stealing beds and food).

## TIP!

The plains have plenty of oak or birch trees, but that doesn't mean you can't find saplings from other biomes and grow them here.

## PRIVATE ISLAND - MUSHROOM FIELDS

Perhaps you've been playing for a while and have decided to start afresh. Maybe on your own private island? Mushroom fields biomes tend to spawn as small islands in the middle of oceans, making them the perfect private getaway.

You could build a huge castle, so it looks like it's bursting out of the sea, or a small, neat cottage with land to breed mooshrooms. A nice bonus to living in mushroom fields is the lack of nasty mobs, as they can't spawn on the ground there.

## THE COOLEST VIEW - ICE SPIKES

One of the coolest scenes - literally - appear in the ice spikes. Huge towers of ice climb upwards from the lakes of ice below and create a wasteland of cold. In between the ice spikes, you'll find patches of snow and plenty of slippery surfaces. It's a cold and lonely place, where the only life you're likely to find are the polar bears.

If you've got a Silk Touch pickaxe you can harvest the ice without it breaking and carry it back home. The ice is perfect for building cool sculptures or structures.

**TIP!**
Due to the cold weather, most water is frozen as ice. You can use torches to keep water from freezing.

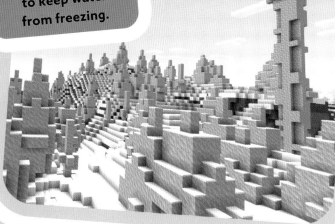

## WATER MEETS LAND - MANGROVES

One of the newer biomes is the mangrove, which often border deserts and jungles, occasionally swamps. The new mangrove tree is only found here and they often grow close together, making walking through the biome quite tricky.

As a lush and warm biome, you'll find tropical fish and glow squid in the bodies of water, while frogs hang out among the tree roots of the mangrove. You won't find many other mobs here, except the bad guys who can often spawn under the leaves of the trees.

As this is a swamp-style biome, the shallow water can provide a great place to gather clay, so don't forget your shovel!

**TIP!**
Mangroves are a great place to find frogspawn which you can scoop up in a bucket to take home and hatch into frogs.

## SOMEWHERE EXOTIC - JUNGLE

Much like forests, the jungle can be tough to explore because of mobs and tightly packed trees. Jungles do offer some really great materials and items for your adventure.

Stalks of bamboo can be harvested and grown to be used in scaffolding, which helps you reach tall places; the only place you'll find melons is on the ground of this leafy paradise; plus, if you enjoy taming animals, there are several types of parrot among the trees.

It can't be tamed, but if you keep your eyes peeled, you may spot an ocelot dashing about in the undergrowth. Due to their close position to water, jungles are often brilliant places to find lots of sugarcane, which is used as sugar in recipes, or converted to paper.

## NEED MATERIALS? - BIRCH FOREST

While forests can prove quite difficult to explore because of the hostile mobs that spawn in the darkness under trees, they can be a great starting point because of the wood. A birch forest contains so many trees it is unlikely you'd ever run out, and wood is a material always used.

You can use shears to trim the leaves, creating a large green canopy to perhaps build a base above the trees; or create a lighter version of the woodland mansion.

There are plenty of other forests out there in the Minecraft world, including the taiga which usually has spruce trees instead of birch.

## TIP!

Wood is a perfect material for a first house, just be careful you don't spill any lava inside!

## UP AND DOWN - EXTREME HILLS

Extreme hill biomes aren't only home to tall mountains, but also plenty of cavernous caves to dive into. This biome is perfect for those who want to build up high and get a good look over the ground below.

The mountains can be used in so many ways; a perfect villain lair can be carved into the side of a mountain; but the ground here can also offer plenty of coal and iron on the surface since the most recent updates.

Keep an eye out for goats who like to roam the clifftops.

## MINERS PARADISE - BADLANDS

The badlands is one of the more rare biomes in Minecraft, but once you've found it you might never want to leave. The mountains here are made of terracotta in layers of different shades, making for perfect building materials.

You won't find trees here as it's so dry, but the badlands feature some unique things to see.

It's quite easy to find abandoned mineshafts here as they're much more common, but you'll also find a crazy amount of gold as it spawns in high numbers.

## HERE COMES A CHALLENGE - UNDERWATER

If you want to set yourself a challenge, particularly towards the end of your adventure, then why not build an underwater base? You could even take over a monument after you've eliminated all the guardians protecting it.

If you explore, you could find some beautiful places to build under the sea. There are colourful coral reefs, deep cold oceans, or shallow lakes to take advantage of. You could build huge glass domes, using sponges to soak up the water; or even create your own sunken ship.

Be careful though, this is difficult due to the limits on breathing while underwater! You can use good enchantments or a conduit to make these projects a little easier, but you'll still need patience while you also deal with the drowned.

**TIP!**
Monuments are a great place to find sponge blocks, which can be used to soak up water if needed.

## HOT AND HUMID - THE DESERT

You could be forgiven for thinking the desert is an empty, boring biome. It looks like that when you first enter, but there's much more to the desert than it seems. The best thing you'll find within the sands is a temple. Loaded with traps, a temple can be explored to find plenty of treasure, or harvested for the sandstone and terracotta.

The desert is the only place to find cactus and various colours of rabbit, and once the sun sets you'll see a variant of the zombie mob as the husks come out to find you.

Deserts are great places to build too. Not only are they quite often flat, but if you use darker materials, you can see your base easily, making it easier to find in a hurry.

# BUILDING YOUR FIRST BASE

Your first base doesn't need to be anything too extraordinary. It's a place to set up as soon as you've spawned into an adventure. You don't need a lot, just enough to get you started and keep the mobs away at night.

## TIP!

If you have dye, you can combine it with your glass to change its colour. Try finding flowers to create basic colours like red, blue or yellow.

## STEP ONE:

Lay down a quick square made from any material you have a lot of, usually this is wooden planks. Make sure your square is made of odd numbers on each side, for example; 7x7 blocks. This means the middle block will be the door.

You can mix up materials to make it look nice as we have in the example. We used jungle and dark oak planks to create a nice base.

## STEP TWO:

From the base, begin to build up and create your walls. You can carry on using different types of wood if you want it to look less plain and boring.

Leave gaps for windows and your door. While you're building up the base, have some sand loaded into your furnace, this bakes it into glass, which you can use for the windows.

Finish off by laying a flat square of planks as your ceiling, then head inside.

## TIP!

While the fence keeps mobs out, it won't stop a creeper from exploding. Make sure you deal with them quickly!

## STEP THREE:

The first thing you need to do inside is place torches. Hostile mobs can't spawn in brightly lit areas, so place a few torches on the walls.

Before placing down any furniture, get your floor laid. It doesn't matter what material you use. We've chosen sandstone which brightens up the inside of the house.

You can now place down your items, such as a bed, some chests, your crafting table and furnaces. We've used some stone to create a little chimney above the furnace.

Now's the time to insert your glass into the gaps you left, to create windows. This helps you see if there are enemies outside before you leave.

## STEP FOUR:

As this is your first base, not only does it need to be a safe place to sleep, it also needs to keep you alive. By using fences, you can split off some land from growing crops and fences will help keep any mobs out, too. You can place torches evenly around to help prevent mob spawns.

You don't need a lot of space to grow wheat, so it's best to start here. Use a wooden or stone hoe to prepare your ground and plant the seeds you get from breaking grass.

Now you've got everything you need built, you can start making it all look better, with a fancy door, or by building up your roof.

# COMPETITION TIME! C

# DO YOU HAVE

# WIN!

We want you to put on your creative hat and build something wonderful in Minecraft. You can use any materials you want, plus you can build it in Creative Mode. We want to see lots of different ideas, using all kinds of blocks. You can build something true to 'real life' or something a bit more wacky and unusual.

Simply send us a screenshot of your build, and the GamesWarrior team will pick their 20 favourite builds to feature in a future GamesWarrior title. So, let's see your best and coolest builds!

## 20 WINNERS WILL GET...

their build published in a future GamesWarrior title!

## PLUS

an advanced copy of the GamesWarrior title with their build inside.

## HOW TO ENTER

**STEP 1**
Take a screenshot of your build.

**STEP 2**
Send your screenshot to competitions@littlebrotherbooks.co.uk by the 31st March 2024.

Use 'Minecraft 2024 Edition Competition' as the subject of the email.

Include your name, age, postal address and contact email address.

You must ask your parent or guardian's permission to enter the competition.

# THE BEST BUILD?

## COMPETITION TERMS & CONDITIONS

# TIPS
## FOR EXPLORING THE
# OVERWORLD

The Overworld is where you'll spend most of your time. Across several biomes, you'll need to explore to find helpful items and materials to craft new weapons and tools, as well as build a home. Even the simplest materials are important in Minecraft, as everything is used to craft bigger and better items.

**TIP!**
Remember, if you break the bed, your spawn changes back to world spawn and not to where the bed was.

### BRING A BED
You already know that a bed will set your spawn point and pass the time overnight. Bringing a bed on long adventures will make sure you never see the dark of night and the monsters that brings. It's also helpful to have it in your hotbar, you can quickly place it and interact with the bed to set your spawn if you find yourself surrounded by enemies in caves or dark areas.

### AND DON'T FORGET THE TORCHES
It's easy to head out on a trip and forget to bring torches, but these little bright spots of light are so important. Not only will they light your way in cave systems, but they can be used to form a trail back home, or back to safety if you need it. Imagine them like breadcrumbs from a fairytale, tracking your journey.

**TIP!**
Redstone torches don't emit enough light to brighten an area, these are only for redstone machinery.

## SAPLINGS ARE YOUR FRIENDS

Always bring an axe on long journeys! Whenever you find yourself in a new biome with different trees, chop down the entire trunk. This makes the leaves slowly break down, dropping sticks and saplings. These saplings can be brought back to your home biome and grown there. You only need one sapling to start off a healthy farm.

**TIP!**
You can use bonemeal to quickly grow trees, as well as other foods and plants.

**TIP!**
If you carry a crafting table with you, you can condense stacks of iron and coal into blocks which can save space on those epic journeys.

## LOOK OUT FOR SURFACE COAL AND IRON

Since recent updates, the spawning of coal and iron has changed a great deal. While you can still find these underground, you're more likely to find it on the surface of mountains and in the entrances of caves.

## CREEPING IN DAYLIGHT

Most mobs only come out at night and will die in sunlight... but not Creepers. Creepers don't care, they'll spawn anywhere and try to find you. Be aware of the sizzling sound they make when they creep up behind you - if you hear this, just run!

**TIP!**
Creepers aren't the only mob that are happy in the sunlight. When you visit a desert, there is a chance to meet a zombie variant called a husk. These zombies don't burn up.

## WATERCLIMBING

A bucket of water is a very handy tool. If you want to explore a very deep cave, simply pour out the water at the entrance and the water will trickle down, all the way to the bottom. You can then use this to slowly sink down to the bottom without taking fall damage. Once you're finished exploring, just swim up the column of water.

# HELPFUL MOBS

In the world of Minecraft there are lots of friendly mobs that can be used to make your adventure easier. Many of them provide food, which is needed for energy; others can help you travel long distances, or defend against enemies. While there are lots of cute animals, like the parrot and panda, they don't often do much more than wander alongside you, or stay at your home base, playing the role of a pet. There are many helpful mobs you should keep a lookout for.

## SHEEP

When killed, sheep will drop mutton, another good source of food. They will also drop wool, which can be used in several crafts, most important of which is the bed. Getting wool for a bed early in your adventure is super important to pass the time overnight safely. Wool can also be used for carpets, or as a fun building block, as it can be dyed many colours.

## PIG

Pigs were initially the only way to travel across the map, other than walking, when Minecraft first came out. You could ride them by placing a saddle on their backs and guide them with a carrot on a stick. Now, their main use is for food, as they drop pork chops when they die.

## COW

Cows are found in many different biomes in large numbers, usually wandering around mooing to each other. These creatures will drop leather and beef when they die. Beef is great food for energy, while leather is used in many crafting recipes. Cows can also be milked by using a bucket on them. When it's drunk, milk will remove effects like Wither, Poison or Mining Fatigue.

## CHICKEN

Of course, chickens are food when killed, however they have more uses than just their bodies for meat. Chickens also drop feathers, which are used to craft arrows. They will also lay eggs that are used in food recipes. It's always helpful to have a little farm of chickens as they have so many helpful uses.

## HORSE

Now we aren't riding pigs around the Overworld because we have horses. There are also donkeys and mules, but horses are perhaps the loveliest. Once tamed, by leaping on their backs until hearts signal they're tame, you can place a saddle on them and ride around from place to place. Horses are much faster than your walking speed, making them super helpful.

## BEE

Bees are a recent addition to Minecraft and they have several uses. Their hives will usually appear on tree trunks - most commonly oak - and the bees will produce honey and honeycomb. Honey acts a lot like milk, in removing effects. Honeycomb is great for making more hives so the bees can be farmed. You can also make blocks of honey, which are both sticky and bouncy.

## FROG

The main use for this new mob is the creation of froglights. Frogs can be found in swamps where you'll also find tadpoles. Tadpoles can be scooped up with a bucket and taken to different biomes where they grow into frogs. There are three types of frog - warm, temperate and cold, depending on which biome they live in. When a frog eats a magma cube, they produce a block of light which can be used just like glowstone.

## WOLF

Wolves are one of the most reliable mobs. Once these creatures are tamed by feeding them bones, they become your companion. Taking a wolf on a journey with you will give you a slight advantage in battles as they will fight enemies alongside you. Be careful though, wolves will eat chickens and sheep, so don't keep them near your farms.

## DOLPHIN

Dolphins are found in deep waters, usually swimming just under the surface. They don't provide any food, but they can do two things - cause you to swim faster and find treasure. If you feed a dolphin some raw cod, they will zoom off to point out something special. You'll need to swim alongside the dolphin until they stop. These creatures can point out monuments, sunken ships, and underwater temples.

## CAT

Cats, other than being really cute, have two ways in which they can help you. Firstly, creepers are terrified of cats and will do everything they can to avoid them. This is great if you have several tame cats around your home, and taming them is as simple as creeping up to them with some raw fish. Another cool trick can be seen if you place your cat on your bed. Once you've slept through the night with a cat next to you, they'll leave you an item as a present.

## LLAMA

Llamas, much like horses, can make for great transport across the world. However, they can also be equipped with chests, which allows you to carry more items and materials around when you're exploring. If you use different colour carpets on your llama it will change the fabric they have draped across their backs.

## VILLAGER

Sooner or later you will stumble across a village. These villages will be home to lots of villagers, each of which has a different role to play. Some villagers will be farmers, others could be blacksmiths or fletchers. You can trade with these villagers and buy some really helpful items that are must-haves for your journey. Villages can spawn in several biomes and they take on a very different look in each place.

## ALLAY

Allays are another new friendly mob. These fairy-type creatures can be found in cages at pillager outposts or within woodland mansions. Allays fly around and can be called to you by you striking a note block repeatedly. Once an allay is near, drop them an item and they will hold it. Once they're holding an item, they will seek out copies of that item in the area. This makes them the perfect helper for when you're breaking down things like trees, or old buildings.

## WANDERING TRADER

The wandering trader is a lot like the villagers, however the trader turns up unexpectedly and at random times. This friendly mob shows up with his two llamas, likely nearby your home base. Every time a new trader appears they will have different products for sale. Paying in emeralds you can walk away with some great items from all across the world, and using the trader is an easy way to get materials you can't easily find.

## IRON GOLEM

These friendly golems will spawn in villages and they're made to keep everyone safe. Any monsters who appear nearby will be bashed and bopped until they die. There is usually only one per village, but you can craft iron golems using four blocks of iron and a jack-o'lantern. If you have a large base, it can be helpful having a few golems strolling around protecting your property.

21

# VILLAGERS AND TRADING

Villages across the world of Minecraft are home to villagers who do much more than wander around saying 'hrrrm' a lot. In fact, they can be incredibly helpful, providing items that will improve everything from fighting, to exploring.

## HOW TO TRADE

Trading is very simple. Just approach a villager and press the 'use' button, this will bring up a menu. On the left are the possible trades in a list; while on the right you can see your inventory and the trading button.

You will need to hover over and select the item you wish to trade for which is shown as the item on the right, with an arrow pointing at it. What you need to hand over for that item, is shown on the left. As you can see, this book is Lure II, it costs 12 emeralds and one book for the trade.

You'll also notice that you can trade materials for emeralds which is the fastest way to earn them. You could, for example, trade sticks to a fletcher for lots of emeralds, which you could then spend with a librarian.

## UPGRADING THE TRADER

Traders have various levels which rise every time you trade with them. This is shown in the bar on the right, underneath the villagers job role. When this progress bar fills you will unlock the level of Apprentice and more trades will unlock. The trader levels rise up to Master unlocking lots of interesting items to trade for.

## TRADER ROLES

There are lots of different roles for traders to take on and each of these is generated by having a trading table nearby. Trading tables are furniture items such as anvils, stonecutters and lecterns.

You can see the full list of roles below:

**Armorer**
**Butcher**
**Cartographer**
**Cleric**
**Farmer**
**Fisherman**
**Fletcher**
**Leatherworker**
**Librarian**
**Stone Mason**
**Shepherd**
**Toolsmith**
**Weaponsmith**

## RANDOM TRADES

Each trader's trade options are completely random. However, if you break their trading table and place it back down, their trades will refresh and change. This stops happening once you've traded with them and their stock is 'locked in'. Advanced players are able to set up areas and create lots of villagers offering helpful trades.

# ATTACKING A PILLAGER OUTPOST

At some point in your journey you're sure to stumble across a pillager outpost. You can't miss them; these tall buildings, usually made from dark oak, stick out and tower above the surrounding area. Outposts are very dangerous due to the number of pillagers inside, but they contain treasure for anyone brave enough to clear them out.

## TIP!

If you get overwhelmed, try running away. Once you get far away they will lose interest and get back to wandering.

## TIME TO GET INSIDE

Once everyone outside has been eliminated, you can enter the tower. These towers are quite cramped and don't offer a lot of space to move around. You will want a strong sword with some enchantments, a diamond sword at the very least. You will need to kill each pillager fast, before they can swarm you.

## SCOUT THE AREA

Around the tower you'll spot several pillagers roaming around. These guys are nasty and can end your day pretty quickly, especially if they gang up on you. Using a bow, it's worth sneaking around and taking out as many pillagers as you can. They will soon spot you, but if you're quick you can eliminate them.

## GET TO THE TOP

You'll get used to fighting the pillagers and can make your way to the very top of the outpost. There will always be a chest waiting for you, but its contents will be random. You can get some rare loot, such as enchanted books of weapons, so make sure you have some space in your inventory.

## WARNING

There will usually be at least one pillager captain on the top floor of the outpost. You can tell the difference as these will have an 'ominous banner' on their backs. Once these pillagers are eliminated they will drop the banner for you to take as a trophy, however, you will be cursed with the Bad Omen effect.

## BAD OMEN

This effect can be dangerous if you don't know how to deal with it. The Bad Omen effect will trigger a raid if you enter a village. A raid is made up of several waves of pillagers, steadily getting harder as they pass. By defeating the entire raid, you can get a Totem of Undying, which will bring you back to life if you die.

If you'd rather not have the Bad Omen effect you can get rid of it by drinking a bucket of milk.

## TIP!

The Totem of Undying must be carried in your offhand (the one that doesn't hold a tool or weapon). If you die, you will instantly return to life as the totem breaks. A totem can only be used once, so choose when to use it carefully.

# PIGLIN BARTERING

Piglins are a mob found in the Nether. They're fussy little guys who have a love of gold. If they spot you're not wearing any gold armour, they will attack you; if they see you digging up gold, they will attack you. However, if you give them gold, they will swap it for a random item.

## TIP!

Baby piglins won't barter any items for gold. They also never grow into adults, which is weird.

## FINDING PIGLINS

Piglins spawn naturally in Nether wastes, crimson forests or bastions. You'll find them wandering around, often alone. Remember, piglins will only attack you if you strike them by mistake, or if they see you opening a nearby chest. If you're in a bastion, the piglins wearing black – brute piglins – will attack you for no reason... so be careful.

## TIME TO BARTER

You can start a barter in two ways; by handing a gold ingot to a piglin by pressing the 'use' button, or you can drop it on the floor in front of them. Either way works and the piglin will pick it up and look at it for a few seconds. Once they're happy, they will drop an item for you as a reward.

## PIGLIN DROPS

The items a piglin drops in a barter is random, however the item pool they choose from isn't too big, so you'll often get something good. Bartering is really helpful for getting things like ender pearls or potions of Fire Resistance. Unlike villagers, piglins never run out of items so you could trade for as long as you want. All it costs is gold ingots, which can be easy to find in mesa biomes in the Overworld.

You can see the full list of piglin drops below:

Enchanted book with soul speed

Iron boots with Soul Speed

Splash potion of fire resistance

Potion of fire Resistance

Water bottle

Iron nugget

Ender pearl

String

Obsidian

Crying obsidian

Fire charge

Leather

Soul sand

Nether brick

Spectral arrow

Arrow

Gravel

Blackstone

## TIP!

Soul Speed is an enchantment on boots that stops you from slow walking while crossing soul sand.

# THE NETHER AND ITS BIOMES

When it comes to visiting the Nether, there are certain things you need to remember. Mostly, that everything in this dimension is trying to end your adventure. If it's not the pools of lava you must avoid, it'll be the monsters blasting you with fiery explosions or hitting you with swords. Much like the Overworld, the Nether has a few biomes and learning about them is key to getting out alive!

## NETHER WASTES

The Nether wastes are kind of like the plains of the Nether. It's the most common biome you'll find and it's relatively safe compared to other biomes. There's little to see in this area except for pigmen, piglins and a few materials.

In the netherrack around the wastes you can find quartz and Nether gold. Quartz is a great building block that can be shaped into different forms using a stonecutter. Nether gold drops in nuggets, but can be combined into gold ingots - be aware of piglins in the area, if they spot you mining the gold, they'll attack you.

The Nether wastes is often broken up by huge lakes of lava. The only way across this molten rock is by building bridges from blocks, or hitching a ride on the back of a strider, who are friendly mobs that live in the lava.

## TIP!

Nether wastes are great because they're quite flat, but this means ghasts can spot you easily. There's not often many places to hide.

TIP!
You can bring warped forest wood back to the Overworld if you want to build with its unique green/blue colours.

# WARPED FOREST

The warped forest of the Nether can be quite a pretty place, if you ignore the lava. It's not too dangerous as the only mobs that spawn there are Endermen. As long as you don't look in their eyes, they won't attack.

It's worth visiting for extra building materials as the trees offer a new colour of wood. Plus, if you can utilise some tactics you could farm Endermen for their ender pearls - a great item that teleports you to where the pearl is thrown. These pearls are also needed to craft items that take you to the Ender Dragon fight at the end of the game.

# CRIMSON FOREST

The crimson forest is rather different to its warped cousin. Not only is this forest red rather than green, but you'll find lots of fungus here. The floor is covered in crimson nylium which can be taken home to use in building, and the trees hold shroomlights which act as light sources in your home.

There are more mobs in this forest, so it's harder to explore. Piglins will attack you if you aren't wearing any gold items; though if you are, feel free to trade with them. What you need to watch out for are the hoglins, the Nether's warthog. These little creatures will headbutt you, which hurts more than you'd think. They will stay away if you're standing close to any warped fungus, but a few whacks with a sword should take care of them. They drop lots of leather, which is great for making books.

TIP!
This is the only biome in the Nether with an readily available source of food, in the form of hoglins.

29

# BASALT DELTA

It's tricky to stay walking in a straight line in the basalt delta. The entire biome is made up of jagged spikes, small pools of lava and sudden drops. You'll want to keep one eye on your feet and another looking for magma cubes.

The delta is a high spawn area for magma cubes. You'll find them hopping about everywhere, often trying to knock you off a pillar and into some lava. It's the perfect place to farm magma cream, or bring along a frog and have them gobble down the smallest magma cubes. This will produce froglights to be used in building.

You'll also find a lot of blackstone here, which, when polished up, makes for a lovely building block. If you make it home safely, that is.

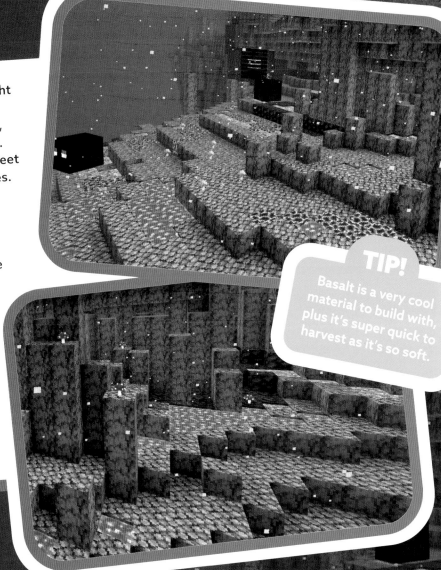

## TIP!
Basalt is a very cool material to build with, plus it's super quick to harvest as it's so soft.

# SOUL SAND VALLEY

These valleys can be extremely dangerous to cross. Not only will the soul sand slow down your walking speed, making you an easier target for ghasts to blast you; but these biomes are usually filled with lava.

There are good reasons to make your way through - ghasts and skeletons spawn here and each drop helpful items. A ghast tear makes for great potions and bones from skeletons are always handy. You will need to be ready to put out fires by hitting them as the soul sand and soul soil catch fire easily. This soul fire hurts a lot more than regular fire, so be warned.

Don't forget to harvest some soul sand if you plan on growing Nether wart. If you already have access to enchantments, a Soul Speed enchantment on your boots will keep you walking at your usual speed on the sand.

# NETHER FORTRESS

**F**ortresses are most often found in the Nether wastes biome. Sometimes they can be very difficult to find as they aren't very common. Tracking one down is very important for adventurers due to what is contained inside a fortress.

You'll need two things for potion making, and both of them are here - Nether wart and blaze rods. If you stumble across a large fortress, they can feel a bit like a maze... a maze filled with horrible monsters. You never know if you're going to run into a skeleton, a blaze, maybe even a wither skeleton.

However, exploring is a must. As you search for Nether wart, you will probably find random chests scattered around which are a good source for golden armour and horse armour. Hopefully you'll find some blazes who drop blaze rods when they die - these rods break down into blaze powder which fuels your brewing stand, to make potions.

# BASTION

**A** bastion is probably the scariest thing in the Nether. It's a huge castle-type structure filled with piglins, lava, open holes and, worst of all, piglin brutes. These brutes can be identified by their black outfits, rather than the brown that normal piglins wear. Brutes will attack you on sight with axes and they hit hard!

Unless you're wearing netherite armour, these fights will be a struggle. They can track you down from anywhere inside the bastion and don't give up. Be prepared.

It's worth exploring a bastion if you can as they're filled with treasure chests. A word of caution: opening a chest will attract all the piglins and they will try to stop you taking their loot. So, more fighting is on your list of to-dos.

Larger bastions can feel like broken labyrinths, with lots of dead ends and holes that drop to lower floors. You never know if you're going to fall down and be ambushed by piglin enemies. Doesn't exactly sound like fun, does it? The loot is worth it, though.

## TIP!

Bastions can be a source of Nether wart if you're struggling to find a fortress. It's also the only place to find the Pigstep music disc.

# EXPLORING UNDERWATER AND MONUMENTS

A big part of Minecraft is exploring. Players often want to see everything the world has to offer them and that includes underwater. Not only are there beautiful fish and dolphins to discover, but also ship wrecks and massive monuments protected by a creature called the guardian. But how do you explore a place so dangerous?

## BREATHING

If you've taken a dip in any water already, you'll notice that you have an air meter when your head goes under. This slowly empties as your character's lungs do. Running out of air soon starts affecting your health and your hearts begin to empty, leading to death.

So, what can you do? There are actually two ways to prevent death by drowning - enchantments, and potions.

Using an enchantment table, or enchanted books, you can apply Respiration to your helmet. It's also worth trying to enchant other armour items with Aqua Affinity which allows you to break blocks faster while underwater.

If you're looking at potions, you will need to brew an Awkward potion, like normal, then add a pufferfish as your main ingredient. This creates a potion of Waterbreathing which will help greatly.

## TIP!

The underwater version of the zombie - the drowned - will hang out in all depths of water. Don't get too close unless you can eliminate them quickly. If a drowned starts throwing tridents at you, get out of the water fast!

## SUNKEN SHIPS

Shipwrecks are waiting for you at the bottom of the ocean. Inside these sunken ships you will find a chest that contains a few valuables and, most importantly, a treasure map. Once you have a map, you can follow it to some buried treasure nearby, giving you even more valuables and also an item called The Heart of the Ocean.

## MONUMENTS

These enormous buildings sit on the seabed and feature a few treasures of their own. However, there's something standing in the way - guardians. These creatures can cause all sorts of problems for underwater explorers. Looking a bit like pufferfish, these green mobs will not only blast you with a laser, causing lots of damage. They will also hurt you if you hit them with a sword as their spiky bodies will stab your character.

Fighting guardians is hard work as you don't have many options. The best tactic is to try and corner them in the monument and rapidly hit them with your sword - just be ready with healing potions when taking damage from the spikes.

You can also use a bow as the arrows shoot faster than the guardian's laser can. Another solid option is the trident. As this weapon comes from the sea, it makes for a good weapon as swinging it isn't as slow as a sword.

## ELDER GUARDIANS

As you reach further inside the monument, you'll come across elder guardians. These are much bigger versions of the creatures and they have a lot more health. Never attempt to fight one unless you have the best armour and a good sword. These mobs can kill you in just a couple of hits.

Tactics for beating them are the same as the smaller guardians, except it will take much longer.

### TIP!

Being in the same area as guardians - even on the surface of the ocean - will apply an effect called Mining Fatigue. With this effect you won't be able to break blocks at your usual speed, it will slow you down hugely. Breaking things, like a placed bed, now takes almost a whole minute.

# WEAPONS

Every Minecraft adventurer needs a good collection of weapons. The only way to battle monsters is to craft great weapons and get them enchanted. Whether you're fighting zombies, or the Ender Dragon, you can trust on your weapons.

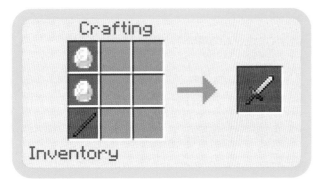

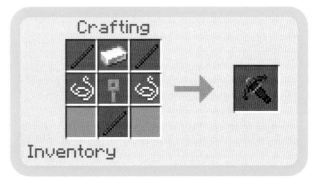

## SWORDS

Swords are always going to be your main weapon of choice, however, an axe can make for a great weapon if your sword suddenly breaks. The best material you can use to craft a sword is netherite, but as it's quite hard to find, diamond is your best bet.

BEST ENCHANTMENT: Sharpness V - Sharpness is better for killing all mobs, which makes it a stronger weapon.

BEST ENCHANTMENT: Infinity - Enchanting a bow with infinity means you will never run out of arrows. As long as you have at least one arrow in your inventory.

BEST ENCHANTMENT: Quick Charge III - Crossbows with the quick charge enchantment will fire much faster, allowing you to shoot more arrows during a fight.

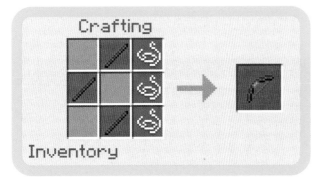

## BOWS AND CROSSBOWS

A bow, or a crossbow, is the perfect back up weapon. You won't always be able to get up close and fight with your sword. Some enemies will linger away from you and will need to be shot with arrows. Either weapon will work and what you use depends on which you prefer.

## TRIDENT

Coming from under the water, literally, is the trident. This isn't a great weapon to use above the water, but if you're fighting drowned or guardians, the trident will attack faster than a sword. It's also a handy way to fly when it's raining.

BEST ENCHANTMENT: Riptide III - Riptide is such a fun enchantment as it lets you fly into the air whenever its raining.

**TIP!**
Tridents cannot be crafted. They are only found when dropped by a drowned.

# TOOLS

Just as important as your weapons are your tools, where would you be without a set of tools? These are needed to harvest materials to craft everything from items to buildings. Your trusty pickaxe is probably the tool you will use the most during your adventure. It's used for mining everything from stone to diamonds.

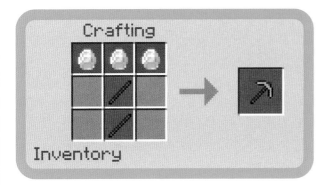

## PICKAXE

One of the first tools you will craft, and the one that will be replaced most often. After all, the game is called Minecraft, so you'll need to do plenty of mining! After you've found a large amount of iron, you'll never need a stone or wooden pickaxe as these can't mine gold or diamonds.

BEST ENCHANTMENT: Fortune III - If you want more gems and ore, then Fortune on your pickaxe will let ore blocks drop more materials.

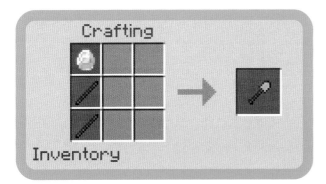

## SHOVEL

Getting through dirt or sand can take time by hand. A shovel is much better equipped for the job. You don't need any fancy materials to make a shovel, but iron ore or diamond will make your shovel last longer.

BEST ENCHANTMENT: Efficiency V - Digging through dirt, gravel or sand will be lightning fast with this enchantment.

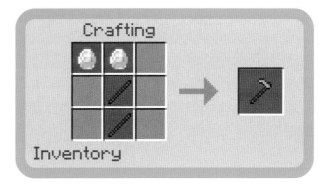

## HOE

As with shovels, you don't need strong materials for a hoe. In fact, you'll probably use it the least out of all the tools. You can get by with a stone hoe for the entire adventure.

BEST ENCHANTMENT: Efficiency V - You can speedily harvest your crops with an Efficiency enchantment.

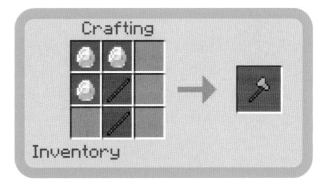

## AXE

You won't build much without access to wood, and the fastest way to chop down trees is with an axe. Better materials mean a longer lasting axe and a slightly quicker chopping speed.

BEST ENCHANTMENT: Unbreaking III - This enchantment will slow down how quickly your tool breaks down.

**TIP!**
One of the best enchantments for all tools and weapons is Mending.

# ANIMAL BREEDING

Keeping animals is a part of setting up a farm. There are many materials you can harvest from animals. It's worth keeping some space near your home in order to set up a small animal farm. You are going to want to keep cows, sheep and chickens.

## WOOLY SHEEP

Wool is used for a few things. The top use is for decorating as the blocks of wool are nice and bright, and they come in a range of colours. Your sheep enclosure must be larger than any other as the sheep will munch the grass in order to grow their fleece again.

If you want different colours, it's better to dye the sheep, rather than white wool. This saves on dye, plus it makes your farm really colourful.

You can make a rainbow sheep who changes colour with this simple tip. Use a nametag on an anvil and write jeb_. Once you put the name tag on a sheep, they will begin to cycle through colours and become a rainbow.

**TIP!**

Fences are the best way to keep your animals in a safe place. Rather than using a gate, which could allow the animals to escape if you're not fast enough, you can place a piece of carpet on top of the fence. This allows you to jump into the enclosure, but the animals can't jump out.

## MEAT AND LEATHER

Having lots of cows around can help you with two things - beef, for filling up your energy; and leather, which is really important for crafting books. Books are a must if you want to set up an enchantment room. You need lots of bookcases and to craft those, you need three books per bookcase.

Leather is also used for item frames which are helpful for displaying what is contained in chests or for displaying your rare items.

## LOOK AT ALL THOSE CHICKENS

Rather than show you another fenced enclosure, we're going to show you a great way to keep chickens which allows you to collect their eggs easily. You're going to build a glass case where the chickens live, with an egg collector underneath.

**STEP 1** - Place two double chests next to each other.

**STEP 2** - Crouch and place four hoppers directly on top of the chests. If you don't crouch, you'll end up opening the chests

**STEP 3** - Still crouching, place four pieces of carpet on top of the hoppers.

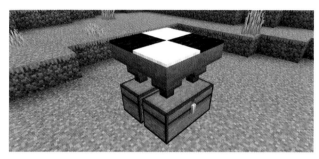

**STEP 4** - Build your glass case around the chests and hoppers, building upwards. You want the top row to be two layers above the carpet. This way the chickens can't escape.

**STEP 5** - Leave a gap in the bottom rows so you can access each chest, as this is where your eggs will end up.

**STEP 6** - Create some steps so you can reach the top of the build.

**STEP 7** - Lure some chickens into the hole using seeds. You only need two as you can breed them while they're in the hole.

**STEP 8** - Add a few torches on the corners to stop mobs spawning, and you're all done!

Check back often to breed more chickens and empty the chests of eggs. If you need feathers or meat, you can kill some of the chickens then breed them again.

# WIZARD TOWER

Once you've been playing for a while, you might want to try your hand at building some more advanced projects. For this build, a wizard tower, we used Creative Mode, but you can easily construct this in Survival if you have the materials you want to use. Feel free to change the colours and materials to those you prefer.

## TIP!

Try to use blocks of precious metals or gems to build, it really changes the look of any building and makes everything look more glamourous.

## STEP ONE:

We always start by building a solid base for our projects. We began this build by placing the floor of chiselled diorite first, so we could get an idea of how big the tower would be.

Using quartz and stripped birch logs, we started to build the walls, using more diorite for the ceiling.

Stairs around the outside makes for a nice detail, and begins the theme of this building growing thinner as it gets taller.

## STEP TWO:

We've jumped ahead quite a bit here, but you can add the next floor by building on top of the ceiling you just placed. Make sure you shrink the room by one block, creating a thinner room.

You can leave spaces for windows as you go.

For the next floor, we shrink the tower once again, but this time use polished copper to make this part of the tower look a little more exciting.

This floor is solid as there is not enough space inside for items.

The spire on the top is quartz column, topped with a lightning rod, just in case of storms.

We've used fences, slabs and lanterns to add nice details to the outside of the tower.

## TIP!

You could add cobwebs and replace some of the quartz in the walls with a different style of block to make this tower look abandoned.

## STEP THREE:

Now it's time to head inside. As this is a wizard tower, we wanted to make the inside look like a potion brewing room.

To do this, we built bookcases and brewing stands, also adding a cauldron to the side of the ladder.

Placing glowstone adds a lovely source of light, as do the red glass windows.

You can see we also crafted some candles to make everything feel a bit more cosy.

## STEP FOUR:

For the upper floor, we added a bed and a double chest. It looked a bit lonely and boring at first, so we added in birch slabs as shelves to hold some more candles.

Make sure you leave a gap for the ladder. You could make the tower a lot wider and create a spiral staircase to the upper floor if you prefer.

# ADVENTURES WITH FRIENDS

**Minecraft supports up to four people when playing multiplayer in the same home. Playing online, you can gather many more people to play together. Playing, and most importantly, creating together is a magical thing.**

## PLAYING ON ONE CONSOLE

If you have friends and family local to you and find yourself playing on console, you can create a multiplayer game easily. Choosing to play multiplayer puts you and your friends into one world where you can build together, craft items for each other and challenge the Ender dragon as a group.

To set up a one console multiplayer world, follow these simple instructions:

- Create a new world as you would normally.
- Uncheck the 'multiplayer' option as this is meant for online play.
- Enter the world.
- Pause the game.
- Have your friends turn on their controllers and choose a profile to use.
- HAVE FUN!

## INVITING YOUR FRIENDS

You can select to 'invite friends' from the pause menu, on the right side panel. In here you can choose a few friends to play with by sending them an invite.

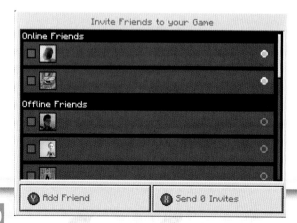

## REALMS

If you prefer to use the internet to play online, you can make use of Minecraft Realms. Realms are a little like servers, where everyone can log in and play whenever they want, rather than having to wait for the host to sign in and play. It doesn't matter the time of day, the realm can be played by anyone.

A realm is a great way to play Minecraft, but it does cost a little money each month. This is because you're paying for Minecraft to host the world for you. Ask a grown-up for permission before purchasing a subscription. A realm can hold up to 10 people playing at once.

To set up a realm, follow these simple instructions:

- Underneath the 'Create New' option will be a button for Realms.
- Select the pencil icon.
- Here, you can play a realm or manage one, if you're setting up a realm, choose 'manage'.
- In this new menu, you can set up your new world, invite friends and manage your subscription payments.
- Choosing to edit your world, you can choose to use resource packs, change the options, difficulty level and the usual options you'd see in a single player world.

## TIP!

Modded Minecraft is a huge community, with hundreds of thousands of mods that change the game completely. Some might change the look of the game, while others can make Minecraft super difficult, or feature collectable dinosaurs and nuclear power plants.

**RLCRAFT**

## JAVA SERVER

A Java server is a lot like Realms, however it is only for playing the Java version of Minecraft, on PC. The reason to choose a server rather than a realm is because of what you can do with a server that isn't possible elsewhere.

For example, a server would allow you to use a modded version of Minecraft, such as Vault Hunters, RLCraft and Dungeons, Dragons and Spaceships to play with friends and family.

Setting up a server is a lot more complicated than a realm, so you'll need a parent or guardian to help. Servers, much like realms, will cost you a little per month. However, a server can hold many more players than a realm can.

**VAULT HUNTERS**

Minecraft Java can only be played on PC. Java is the original version of the game, created in 2011.

# MINING DIAMONDS

Finding diamonds is usually the first big milestone in a Minecraft adventure. Until much later in the game, diamonds are the strongest material you can use for weapons, tools and armour. So, it's quite important that you know how to find them, harvest them safely and make the most of them once you've got some.

## FINDING DIAMONDS

Diamonds are found very deep into the ground. Since the Caves and Cliffs update, which extended the depth of worlds, diamonds are found the most on layer -59. This is the middle digit of your coordinates. Once you've mined your way down to this layer, you can set up a strip mine and begin to look for the precious gems within the deepslate rocks.

### TIP!

In the settings of your game, you will find an option to turn on coordinates. This is very helpful for finding out which layer of the world you are currently on.

## STRIP MINING

This mining technique is the most popular, but also a big time saver compared to mining randomly. Strip mining allows you to see more of the layers with less digging. Using the image below, you can see how to quickly and easily set up a mine.

Your strip mine corridors need to be two blocks high, which is the height of your character. As you mine forwards, you will be able to see the layer above you, plus the layer under your feet. These are along with the walls, of course. Mining in this way means you'll see six blocks around your avatar at the perfect level for diamonds.

Your next corridor, once you've mined forwards enough, will be two blocks width away from your first corridor. You'll always be able to see everything in the four layers around you.

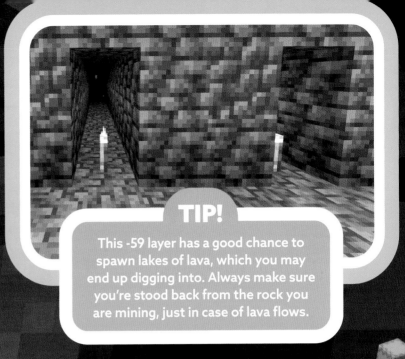

### TIP!

This -59 layer has a good chance to spawn lakes of lava, which you may end up digging into. Always make sure you're stood back from the rock you are mining, just in case of lava flows.

### TIP!

When you find diamonds, it's always worth mining out the rock around the diamonds first, especially if they're in the floor. This stops any possible lava puddles from burning up your gems if they happen to fall in.

## GETTING MORE DIAMONDS

The fastest way to harvest more diamonds is by using an enchantment called Fortune. Fortune comes in three levels - the higher the level, the better Fortune will perform. Basically, what it does is multiply the number of diamonds you can harvest. For example, diamond ore will only drop one diamond when mined with a basic tool. However, with Fortune applied, diamond ore could drop up to four diamonds.

If you're out hunting, try to get the best Fortune enchantment possible. Fortune also applies to every other ore, so you'll walk away with more than normal.

### TIP!

A diamond pickaxe is required to harvest obsidian, which is used to craft a portal to the Nether. Using any other type of tool will cause the obsidian to break.

## CRAFTING WITH DIAMONDS

Now you have diamonds you can start crafting. Diamond is a tough material so any tools or weapons you craft will last much longer. Diamond tools will also harvest materials faster than iron or stone.

To get a full set of armour, you will need 24 diamonds; a sword needs 2 diamonds and your tools will require 1 to 3 diamonds, but usually players only craft a pickaxe which requires 3 diamonds.

# CHALLENGES

There is so much to do in Minecraft. Over the years more and more has been added to the game to offer players extra things to do. A fun way to work through the game and see all the cool things, is to set yourself challenges. Or, in this case, we're going to set them for you. Some of these challenges are inspired by advancements and achievements, so you'll unlock a few of those as we go.

## 1 BUILD THREE BASES

Our first challenge will tackle your creativity. You need to build three different bases, but there's a catch, one must be on the ground, one in the air and the third should be underwater. If you want to take it further, you could build a base in the Nether, too.

## 2 BE A ZOMBIE DOCTOR

Every so often you'll find a zombie villager. These poor souls are destined to wander the map unless you help them. Lure one back to your home and throw a splash potion of Weakness at them. While they're under that effect, feed them a golden apple, and hey presto, a cured villager!

ENDER DRAGON

ZOMBIE DOCTOR

## 4 THE END... AGAIN...

It's time to respawn the Ender Dragon. That's right, once you've beaten the dragon once, sh can be resurrected to fight again. For this, you need End crystals and these must be placed on the portal i the End where you fought her before.

Here's the recipe and how you must arrange the crystals:

## 3 HOT TOURIST DESTINATIONS

Is this one easy? Or a difficult task? We want you to visit all five of the Nether biomes. To track your progress, the list below will help.

- Basalt Delta
- Crimson Forest
- Nether Wastes
- Soul Sand Valley
- Warped Forest

## 5 VERY VERY FRIGHTENING

It's your task to strike a villager with a lightning bolt. Yeah, it's not very kind, but it's part of the fun. You must be the one to cause the lightning strike and to do this, you must have a trident with the Channeling enchantment. Then get out there and bop a villager with the power of electricity.

**SHEEP BREEDING**

## 6 EAT EVERY FOOD

Hope you're hungry! You may think this is an easy challenge, but there are 40 foods that require eating. This includes foods such as glow berries which can only be found in lush caves; pufferfish which will make you sick; and an enchanted golden apple, which must be found in the world as it can't be crafted.

## 7 BREED EVERY ANIMAL

This one will have you travelling the world looking for pairs of animals. You have to breed every single different animal. Don't worry, you aren't required to take them home, so you can breed them in the wild. Some of these will be tough, particularly the striders, and the ocelots.

## 8 DEFEAT THE WITHER

If you thought the Ender Dragon was tough, then you haven't seen anything yet. The Wither is a very dangerous and nasty boss. To spawn the Wither, you need four blocks of soul sand and three wither skulls. The skulls are rare drops from wither skeletons in Nether fortresses. The Wither flies around firing explosive fireballs at you and it does tremendous damage, while destroying the blocks around you. Good luck!

**THE WITHER**

## 9 BRING HOME THE BEACON

Now we're getting to some of the really tricky ones. You need to build a beacon. This is difficult because to craft a beacon, you need a Nether star which you get from defeating the Wither boss. But, you just did that, right?

Here's the recipe for the beacon, and how to set it up:

## 10 CREATE A MUSEUM

This one's just for fun, but it will also challenge everything you know about Minecraft. It's time to build a museum dedicated to the game. The building can be as big as you need it to be, but you must represent every single block, item, animal and biome. Use item frames, fancy materials to display your blocks and include flowers and plants for decoration.

**BEACON**

# LOOKING TO THE FUTURE

The most recent update to Minecraft brought with it a lot of changes to the game's deserts. For a long time, the desert only featured villages and empty temples. Update 1.20, also known as Trails & Tales has a lot in store for players.

## NEW MOBS

Trails & Tales brings two brand new passive mobs to Minecraft, one of which was chosen by the community.

First up is the camel which can carry two players to ride through the desert. These big beasts are very cool, they have a dash ability which makes them move in a swift rush of energy. It's perfect for crossing small gaps.

Next is the community vote winner, the sniffer. This colorful mob was once extinct in the world of Minecraft, but their eggs can be found via a new feature, archeology. Once hatched, the sniffer looks a bit like a fluffy turtle. Sniffer's can smell ancient seeds in the ground, which you can then plant and harvest.

## ARCHEOLOGY

Around desert temples you will be able to find suspicious sand. By using the new brush tool on this sand you'll unearth pottery shards, hidden tools and much more. There are lots of shards to find and plenty of those sniffer eggs, too.

## ARMOUR TRIM

With the 1.20 update, players are able to use smithing templates found throughout the world to customise armour. No longer will your armour look plain and boring, as you can add new coloured patches and stand out to your friends.

## MORE FOR THE BUILDERS

This latest update brings so much for those who love to build. These new blocks will allow for new styles and colours to be used when crafting those huge buildings or structures.

## BAMBOO AND BLOSSOM

As you can see in our picture, there is now more to do with bamboo; you can craft two building blocks from it. There are also cherry blossom trees to be found throughout the world and they can be harvested into planks, stairs, doors and more.

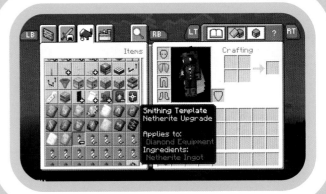

Bamboo can now also be used to create a raft for sailing the oceans and rivers.

## ACCESSORIES

You can also see that new signs are available, which hang from surfaces, ideal for role-players who enjoy running shops in villages. There will also be a chiseled bookshelf that can store six books and it acts as a redstone signal, like a switch or button. Now we can all finally construct a library with a secret door accessed by pushing a book onto a shelf!

# MINECARTS AND RAILS

Minecarts and rails are a handy way of transporting yourself, or items, across long distances. By using iron, gold, wood and redstone, you can construct tracks down into your mine; you can make routes between your house and your friend's homes, too.

## THE CARTS

There are four different minecarts available to use; the standard cart transports people; there's a chest cart to move materials; a hopper cart for complex farms and machinery; and lastly, a TNT cart, which can be sent into caves to explode from a distance.

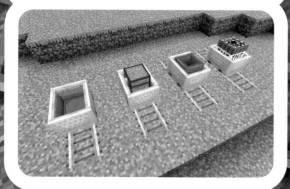

These redstone lamps will light up as the minecart travels over the detector rails in the middle.

## THE RAILS

There are also four types of rail for use in track laying. There's a standard rail; a powered rail which boosts the speed of carts; a detector rail which sends a red stone signal; and there's the activator rails which will set off the TNT cart, or eject people.

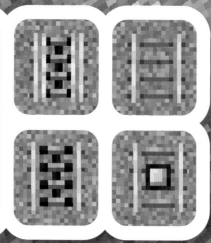

Powered rails will give a boost of speed to the cart, but they must be powered by placing a redstone torch next to the rails.

The buttons you see on the detector rails are switches that send an electric signal to the lamps.

Redstone torches are simple to craft, from redstone dust and a stick, these create a point of electricity.

Powered rails must be used before an uphill section of track, otherwise the cart will be too slow to travel. Powered rails cannot be used as corner pieces of a track.

## EXAMPLE BUILD

To show off what you can do with Minecarts and rails, we've created a small circuit in Creative Mode, which you can copy to see how it works. This is a simple track with some up and down sections, along with some light up redstone lamps.

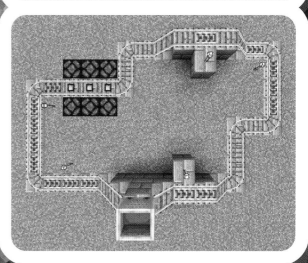

## TIP!

Minecarts can be used to move animals, or even villagers, to new areas. They are also used in more complex situations like creating automatic farms.

# MINECRAFT DUNGEONS

**With Minecraft being such a popular world to experience, more games joined the series. Minecraft Dungeons is a dungeon crawler where players can team up with friends or play solo to grab loot and become a powerful hero.**

### DOWN IN THE DUNGEONS

While dungeons aren't a big focus of Minecraft, this spin-off game concentrates on using the biomes to cover maps filled with enemies and treasures. The game is based on a type of videogame called an 'ARPG' or Adventure Role-Playing Game.

The idea is to explore and fight through each map looting chests and increasing your character's weapons and abilities. The more powerful you become, the more dungeons unlock and suddenly you're facing huge beasts and scary sorcerers.

The more you play, the more powerful items, weapons and armour you will discover.

Minecraft Dungeons works really well when playing on your own, but you can pull in a few friends either online or on one console to explore together. You don't even need to argue over who gets the loot, as the game works this out for you.

With lots of paid DLC (downloadable content) there are hundreds of hours waiting for you in the dungeons.

# MINECRAFT LEGENDS

**Another entry in the Minecraft series, released more recently, is Minecraft Legends. This new videogame allows players to discover new ways to battle enemies and save the world of Minecraft once again.**

### LEGENDS ARE MADE

The piglins have escaped the Nether and are running riot across the Overworld! The only way you can defeat the piglins and send them packing, is to team up with unlikely allies.

In Minecraft Legends, those mobs you've been fighting for years have now become a part of your team. You can work together with skeletons, creepers and zombies to hopefully ruin the plans of the evil piglins.

This title plays very differently from others as it's a strategy game. You control a character who can command small parties of allies to destroy buildings, fight evil mobs and capture resources. Players can travel across the familiar biomes putting an end to the piglin's destruction.

Minecraft Legends can be played with friends, but it also features a PvP (Player Vs Player) game mode where you can use the tactics you've learned against other players. This competitive mode will decide who the best army captain is.

# MINECRAFT
## MARKETPLACE

The Minecraft Marketplace offers great ways to change the game and make it more your style. It's here where you can buy worlds filled with new themes and adventures, and packs full of great looking skins and textures to give your game a whole new look.

Buying items in Marketplace cost minecoins, so ask a grown-up for permission before purchasing content.

### MINECOINS
Everything in the Marketplace costs Minecoins, a currency created for Minecraft. These coins can only be spent within Minecraft and other games from this world such as Dungeons and Legends. Minecoins cost 'real world' money via a debit or credit card, so make sure you get permission from a responsible adult when buying Minecoins.

**TIP!**

There is a search function in the top-right corner of the Marketplace. You can enter anything you want in here and the shop will search for any content related to your search.

### FRONT PAGE
On the front page of the Marketplace you'll see a lot of new things, and it can be overwhelming. Across the top of this page are the most popular items, as well as all the new additions. Below this rotating section are some buttons pointing to the different sections; Skin Packs, Worlds, Textures & More, and New.

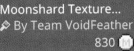

**Moonshard Texture...**
By Team VoidFeather
830

**Tie Dye – Texture Pack**
By The Craft Stars
830

**Ocean Depths Mash-up**
By MelonBP
★ 4.2     660

**Mythical Creatures...**
By Ready, Set, Block!
★ 4.4     1170

**Captive Survival**
By AquaStudio
830

**One Block – Tycoon**
By Aurrora
2040

**Blocky Boo**
By Shapescape
★ 4.6     990

**Parkour Egg**
By Hielke Maps
★ 4.6     310

## TEXTURES & MORE

Texture packs are a quick way to completely change the look of Minecraft. If you've been playing Minecraft for a long time, maybe you're a bit bored of seeing the same old blocks. Now you can see what the world would look like if it was a modern city, or if everything was made out of plastic. There are texture packs that transform your world into ancient Greece, or into orbit and onto a space station.

## WORLDS

The Worlds page lets you play Minecraft in completely new ways. With these add-ons you can find new biomes, classic challenges, horror maps, huge dragon cities, and so much more. Lots of these additions will give you new blocks to play with, or fun challenges for you and your friends, and there are even adventures designed around new ideas. If you want dinosaurs or spaceships in Minecraft, here's your chance.

**Blue Billionaires**
By Tristan...
310

**Power Ninja Skins**
By GoE-Craft
310

**Modern Friends!**
By Asiago Bagels
310

**Funky Icons**
By Team Visionary
490

**Neon RGB**
By Builders Horizon
★ 4.8     490

**Dark Depth Mobs**
By Hourglass Studios
★ 4.8     310

**Neon Demons**
By Giggle Block...
★ 4.8     310

**Pro VS Misfit**
By inPixel
★ 4.8     310

## SKIN PACKS

Skins are the outfit your character wears in-game. You'll start off with Steve, Alex and their friends, but if you want something more fun or exotic, this is the section for you. You can find anything from cool skins made by community members, to packs that crossover with movies or TV shows.

# BEST SKINS

Skins don't alter your game play, they only change the look of your character. Ask a grown-up for permission before purchasing skins.

If you're going to play at your best, you might as well look your best! Minecraft offers lots of options for changing your skin; through the marketplace, or if you're using Java, you can upload skins from popular websites.

### GLOW HORNS · 490 MINECOINS · 12 SKINS
If you want to step out into a neon nightlife you will want these skins. Nothing says 'let's have a party' more than these pink and cyan mashups. Party on!

### CUTE GLITCHES · 490 MINECOINS · 12 SKINS
It's time to get corrupted and glitch out with your friends. These glitch skins use bright, eye-catching colours and super cute expressions to let you really show off your personality.

### MODERN TEENS · 490 MINECOINS · 12 SKINS
Classic style is on the menu with these pastel coloured skins. These cute outfits will let you stand out in the wild world of Minecraft as a modern fashion icon.

### ALIEN GANG · 310 MINECOINS · 10 SKINS
They've come from the far-flung corners of outer space! Nobody is getting abducted as these aliens are here to play. You can take on their form and become part of the gang.

## SPRING FAMILY · 490 MINECOINS · 13 SKINS

If you want bright and colourful, look no further than the Spring Family. You can dress up as a bumble bee, a cloud spilling a rainbow, or a fluffy chick bursting from its egg.

## TEEN ROBOTS · 310 MINECOINS · 12 SKINS

Bzzzt! It's time to oil those hinges and get mechanical with this skin pack of teenage robots. Their colourful style makes for a futuristic look when you're mining for diamonds.

## BLACK AND WHITE · 490 MINECOINS · 10 SKINS

Stepping back in time, you can wipe all colour from your outfits and take on a retro look. These black and white skins feel as if they stepped out of the page of a newspaper.

## CUTE ANIMALS · 310 MINECOINS · 20 SKINS

Becoming a cute and cuddly animal might be your dream. Do you want to live a lazy life where humans run around after you making sure you have plenty of food?

## HALLOWEEN HORRORS · 490 MINECOINS · 12 SKINS

We all like being spooked occasionally, right? Sometimes it's good to be the monster. Why not grab a scary skin and hide in your friend's house, ready to give them the surprise of their life?

## DEEP SEA CREATURES · 490 MINECOINS · 10 SKINS

Living at the bottom of the ocean are these creatures - some cute, others a bit more monstrous. If you're after a skin that will match your new underwater base, you'll find it here.

# ENCHANTING

**Enchanting your tools and weapons can give you an edge when fighting or harvesting materials. Setting up an enchanting area is nice and simple, and definitely worth the time. Grab some books, some precious materials and get enchanting!**

### THE TABLE AND THE ROOM

An enchanting table requires some materials that are harder to find - diamonds and obsidian. Once you have these you can create your table, however to get the best enchantments, you will need to create a library around the table, as you can see below. The bookshelves must be placed 'two high' and form the shape you see in the image.

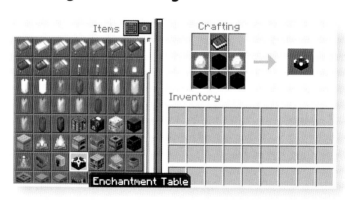

### TIME TO ENCHANT

To use the table, press the use button and you'll see a screen with a few options. Placing in the item you want to enchant, and some lapis lazuli, you will see three enchantment options. The bottom enchantment, which costs more XP and lapis will always be the best enchantment option. Clicking the option will apply the enchantment.

### TIP!

Enchantment selections are random. If you don't like any of the options, place a book into the table instead of a tool or weapon and the enchantment will be placed on the book. This then refreshes the enchanting option for your tool or weapon.

# POTIONS

Potions are a great way of improving your characters abilities. For example, you can use a potion to prevent you dying in lava; or a potion to let your character breathe underwater. There are many potion effects to try and there are only a few steps before you become a brewing pro.

## GATHER YOUR TOOLS

The first step is crafting a brewing stand. In order to do this, and to brew potions, you need some materials from the Nether - blaze rods and Nether wart. These can be found in Nether fortresses. Once you have them craft your station and place it in your home.

**TIP!**

You can grow Nether wart back in the Overworld, you just need some soul sand. Simply place the soul sand and plant the Nether wart.

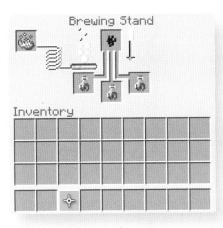

## BREWING POTIONS

Before you open the brewing menu, use a crafting table to turn your blaze rods into blaze powder, this is the fuel for the brewing stand. Now, open the table and place your powder in the correct box. Next, place three bottles of water in the lower section of the stand.

All that's left to place is the Nether wart, which goes into the ingredient box at the top. Let that brew and you'll end up with Awkward potions.

This is the base to every potion in the game. For any potion, you start with an Awkward potion in the bottom. Then you can place other ingredients in the top box to apply the potion effect. For example, magma cream creates Fire Resistance potions, and phantom membranes create Slow Falling potions.

Why not experiment with ingredients and see what you come up with?

**TIP!**

Once you've added your effect you can alter the potion again. Adding glowstone dust will extend the time the effect lasts. While adding gunpowder creates a Splash potion, which can be thrown to add the effect.

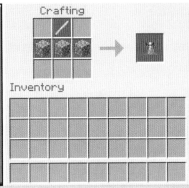

# FARMING TIPS

## TIP!
You can use bonemeal to speed up the growth of your crops. Bonemeal comes from bones which skeletons drop, or can be made in a composter. Simply use it on your crops to see quick growth.

Harvesting food is an important aspect of Minecraft as you have a hunger bar which needs to stay full. Any activity, whether it's fighting or mining, requires energy that comes from your hunger bar. If this empties and you can't fill it, you'll begin to lose health. Farms are a great way to ensure food is always available.

## WHAT TO GROW
The easiest crop to grow, at first, is wheat. Wheat seeds can be found by chopping down stalks of grass across the biome. These seeds can be planted to grow wheat, which is used to craft bread. As you begin to explore you'll find more crops in villages, random chests and exotic biomes.

## TYPES OF FOOD

**WHEAT**

**BEETROOT**

**POTATO**

**CARROT**

**MELON**

**PUMPKIN**

**SWEET BERRIES**

## HOW TO GROW

There are a few ways to set up your farm, but before you start you'll need a hoe. Any material will do as they don't get used often enough to break down. A stone hoe is perfect. When holding a hoe, pressing the 'use' button on grass blocks will prepare the soil for planting.

## SOIL BLOCKS

These soil blocks need to be close to water to make the crops grow at a good speed. Without water, they grow slowly. In the two images below, you can see different ways to set up your farm; in rows, or around a water source.

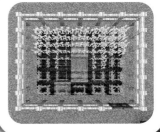

## GROWING SPACE

Which you choose depends on space near your home. Each of these farms makes sure that the crops are growing within two spaces of water. The basic crops -wheat, potato, beetroot and carrot - will grow nicely in this arrangement.

## PUMPKINS AND MELONS

The big change comes with melons and pumpkins. These don't need to be close to water, but they need space as these crops will grow in a random direction - up, down, left or right - from where it's planted. Both pumpkins and melons take much longer to grow than simple crops.

# HOSTILE MOBS

Hostile mobs can prove to be a thorn in your side. They can appear anywhere, but mostly come out at night. Night-time is a dangerous time to be out exploring as spiders will drop on you from trees, skeletons will fire arrows at you from far away, and zombies shuffle endlessly forwards. Never get too cosy, there's always a chance for a mob to get you.

### ZOMBIE
Zombies are undead monsters that will attack you if you get too close. They move slowly, so you can back up if you need space to fight them. Zombies burn in sunlight, unless they're the husk version who live in deserts.

### SKELETON
Skeletons won't fight you up close as they use a bow and arrow to attack. They're very accurate and each arrow will knock you backwards. If you can't run up close or hide from the arrows, you're likely to die quickly.

### CREEPER
Creepers are probably the most well-known mob from Minecraft. If you don't see a creeper, you'll know that they're behind you when you hear a short 'pssst' sound, before they explode.

### SPIDER
Spiders will ignore you in the daytime, but once the sun sets they're happy to crawl close and bite. Spiders drop string, which is useful for crafting bows and fishing rods. Spiders can climb fences and walls, so hiding is no use.

### ENDERMAN
These will attack you if you look them in the eye and have a special ability - teleporting. When they aren't zipping about trying to kill you, they'll pick up random blocks and move them around to confuse you.

### DROWNED
The underwater zombie is one of the most dangerous. They swim fast and will throw tridents at you. Think of this like firing arrows underwater. They hurt! If you manage to find a trident of your own, it will allow you to fly briefly.

### SLIME
Slimes only spawn in wide open spaces, splitting into smaller versions of themselves when eliminated. Slimes drop slime balls when defeated and these balls can be used to make leads and sticky pistons.

### WITCH
Witches are commonly found in swamps, but can spawn elsewhere at night. You'll know a witch is nearby when you hear their grunts, or when they smack you in the head with a potion to poison you.

### WITHER SKELETON
Wither skeletons can apply the Wither effect if they hit you, which will slowly remove your hearts if you can't find safety and recover. They drop bones and coal often, but also have a rare drop of a wither skull.

### GHAST
Kind of a large flying ghost that cries constantly, ghasts can be a real pain. These mobs shoot exploding balls of fire at you. These balls of fire will burn you and the explosion will destroy nearby blocks.

### BLAZE
This mob is only found in Nether fortresses. They hover above the ground, spinning like a tornado of fire. If they spot you, they will shoot small fireballs that can burn you and take away several hearts if you aren't wearing good armour.

### ZOMBIE PIGMEN
These zombies will ignore you for the most part. They wander around doing very little. However, if you accidentally hit one while you're exploring or mining, then every zombie pigman in the area will swarm to you and try to kill you.

### PIGLIN
Piglins love gold but will ignore you if you're wearing a piece of armour made from gold, however if you forget it, they'll attack you as soon as they spot you. You can drop gold ingots in front of a piglin and they will swap it for a Nether item.

### MAGMA CUBE
These cubes of lava bounce around the Nether much like slimes in the Overworld. They break apart when destroyed and drop an item called magma cream, which is used to create Fire Resistance potions.

### PHANTOM
These only spawn if your character has not slept for a few days. They circle overhead and swoop down to attack you. They hurt a fair bit, but can be banished by sleeping. They also drop phantom membranes, which are used to repair elytra.

## DANTDM

DanTDM is one of the most popular Minecraft creators in the world. Coming from the United Kingdom, Dan has been known to create thousands of videos in the world of Minecraft; from challenges to simple adventuring 'let's play' videos.

DanTDM currently has over 26 million subscribers and has created over 3,500 videos.

## JELLY

Dutch YouTuber Jelly has become known for his Minecraft challenges, as well as playing modded multiplayer games.

Jelly currently has over 22 million subscribers and has created over 5,600 videos.

# YOUTUBERS

For so many years, Minecraft and YouTube have been a match made in heaven. Hundreds of thousands of players have set up YouTube accounts to teach others how to play, or simply show off what they can do in the game. With so many to choose from, who could you be watching?

## CAPTAINSPARKLEZ

American Minecraft creator CaptainSparklez uses Minecraft in very unique ways, including creating music videos in-game. More recently CaptainSparklez has been playing one of the most difficult versions of Minecraft, a hardcore playthrough of a mod called RLcraft.

CaptainSparklez currently has over 11 million subscribers and has created over 5,400 videos.

## LDSHADOWLADY

Also known as Lizzie D, this British YouTuber has been creating videos for over 11 years. She has most recently been playing Minecraft on an SMP server (survival multiplayer) with her husband and several other YouTubers. She also has several series based on Minecraft.

LDShadowLady currently has over 6 million subscribers and has created over 1,000 videos.

## STAMPYLONGHEAD

Stampylonghead, also known as Stampy Cat, has been a popular member of the Minecraft YouTube community for years. He became well known for his 'lovely world' where he would create everything from gorgeous structures, to complex redstone machines.

Stampylonghead currently has over 10 million subscribers and has created over 3,500 videos.

## IBALLISTICSQUID

Squid has been a long-time partner of stampylonghead and a successful British YouTuber. Squid is known for his humour and his challenge videos, but has also played a great deal of modded Minecraft.

iBallisticSquid currently has over 4 million subscribers and has created over 2,000 videos.

## DREAM

Dream has become a household name for his Minecraft videos, and for his long-time covering of his face (recently uncovered). Playing with his close group of friends, Dream found fame with his Manhunt videos and his attempts at breaking Minecraft world records.

Dream currently has over 31 million subscribers and has created over 110 videos

## APHMAU

Taking a different approach to playing Minecraft, Aphmau is a creator who uses the game to role-play to build cool structures. Her role-play videos have been watched by millions of people for the comedy she captures.

Aphmau currently has over 16 million subscribers and has created over 4,000 videos.

## TECHNOBLADE

Sadly Technoblade passed away recently after living with cancer. During his time on YouTube he became known for his Skyblock playthroughs and several challenge videos. His SMP adventures are brilliantly funny and clever, and worth exploring.

Technoblade has over 16 million subscribers and has created over 980 videos.

# REDSTONE TIPS

Redstone is an interesting feature of Minecraft. On its own, redstone looks like a pile of red dust. When used in the right way, redstone has great uses. Essentially, it's an electrical system that can be used to control objects or build machines, and it all starts with some red dust.

## THE BASICS

Redstone is found in the lower layers of your world. It can be found in clusters and the ore block will give off light if struck with a tool. When broken, the ore block drops piles of dust which can be used in several items:

## REDSTONE TORCH

The torch acts like a power output. A bit like an infinite battery. Combining redstone into a block will also act in this way

## REDSTONE DUST

If you trail a line of redstone dust it acts like wiring in a machine, carrying the electrical signal. This dust can also receive signals from pressure plates, switches and buttons.

In our example here, you can see we've connected a simple switch to a piston with a line of redstone. This creates a very basic machine. When the switch is flipped it sends an electric signal through the dust and to the piston which then pushes outwards.

Using these items, you can create anything you could possibly imagine. Players in the community have built secret doors, gardens that harvest themselves, giant calculators and so much more. There are lots of tutorials across the internet and simple experiments can be found on YouTube.

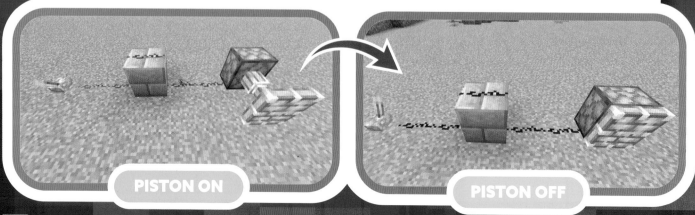

PISTON ON          PISTON OFF

# MAKING A HIDDEN DOOR

Follow along with us and create a hidden door that opens automatically.

**STEP 1**

Place six sticky pistons, leaving a 4 block gap between them. Place a material on the sticky plates, this must match the wall where the door goes. On the middle pistons, add two blocks with a redstone torch below. You also need some redstone dust on top of these blocks.

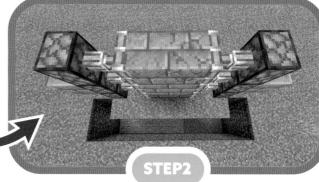

**STEP2**

Dig a trench 3 blocks deep, exactly as it's shown in the image.

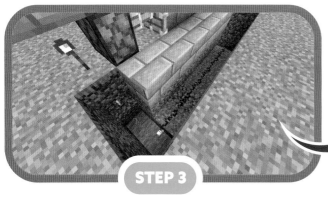

**STEP 3**

Add 5 blocks into the trench with a line of dust on top. At the ends of this new layer, place two redstone torches. From here, you'll need a bit more dust which leads under a block, with another torch on top.

**STEP 4**

Underneath your door blocks, create a 2x4 trench and add redstone dust throughout.

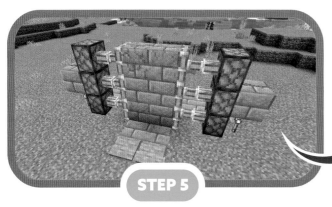

**STEP 5**

Cover the trenches with blocks of your choice, and add four pressure plates following our placement.

**STEP 6**

You can now begin to change the ground blocks and add a surround to match the walls and door.

If you've followed our steps correctly, your pressure plates will be directly placed above the redstone dust. Stepping on a plate sends a signal through the dust, up onto the dust on the raised trench and to the torches. The signal then climbs onto those original blocks we placed on the pistons, which activates them, opening the door.

# MINESHAFT EXPLORATION

Scattered across the world, hidden away in different biomes, are abandoned mineshafts. These mineshafts are left behind by explorers long gone from Minecraft. You can explore freely, and find lots of treasures, but mineshafts can be complex and difficult to navigate.

## EXPLORING THE MINESHAFT

Mineshafts can go up and down through layers; left and right through the rock and dirt, often running into dead ends. Sometimes wooden planks make bridges across ravines, often they line the corridors like pillars. You'll see rail tracks across the floor, broken up and in pieces. Occasionally there will be chest mine carts filled with loot, other times you can enter a corridor and find it clogged with spiderwebs and cave spiders waiting to pounce.

Make sure you have plenty of inventory space as you're likely to fill it up.

### EXPLORING CHECKLIST:
DIAMOND PICKAXE
IRON SHOVEL
3 X STACKS OF COBBLESTONE
2 X STACKS OF TORCHES
PLENTY OF FOOD
2 X BUCKETS OF MILK

## PLOTTING YOUR ROUTE

Because mineshafts are maze-like, you need a way to track where you've been. This way you don't double back on yourself. Use torches to show where you've been - place them on the floor so you don't get confused with those already on the walls. You can use cobblestone to block off corridors with dead ends, or those you have already looted.

## WHAT CAN YOU FIND?

There is plenty of ore to find in these abandoned mineshafts. Iron ore and gold ore can be found in the surfaces of the walls. Mineshafts can sometimes run through lush caves, so there will be moss, dripstone and glow berries to be found.

Treasures are left behind in minecarts, some of which will be useful to farmers as there can be seeds and name tags for animals. You'll find the odd diamond too.

Of course, these mines are long abandoned and now home to monsters. You'll find lots of zombies and skeletons hunting through the shadows, but the worst are the spiders. Long corridors filled with webs are a sign of cave spiders. These are smaller than regular spiders and they poison you when they attack. You can remove the poison by drinking milk.

## TIP!

You can change out torches for flowstone, and the cobblestone for polished granite, to make them stand out even more. These items never spawn in mineshafts, so you'll know you've been there before.

## TIME TO LEAVE

When you feel like it's time to leave, hopefully you will be able to follow your torches out. If, however, you found yourself confused which is so easy to do, you can dig your way out.

Simply choose a solid wall and start digging a staircase upwards. Go slowly, so you can react if you end up digging into lava or water, and eventually you'll be back in the overworld. This isn't an ideal escape route, but it can help when you're feeling lost.

67

# BEATING THE
# ENDER
# DRAGON

For many players, beating the Ender dragon is the final step in this amazing adventure. The dragon is a brilliant beast who lives in the End, patrolling the void surrounded by Endermen. Defeating her in battle is not easy, but if you're prepared for the fight, you should be able to secure the win!

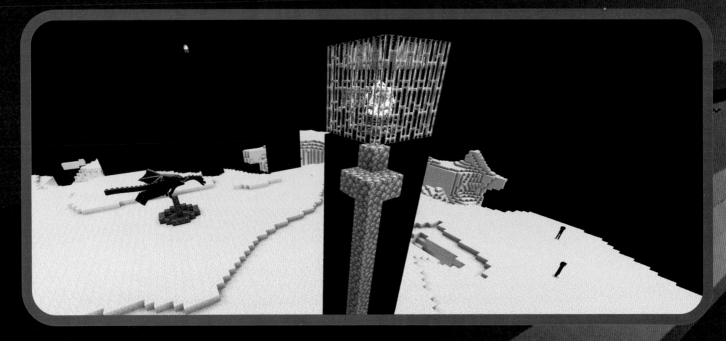

## WHAT TO BRING

You don't need a lot to defeat the Ender dragon, after all, you've been preparing for this moment from the very start of your adventure. With the following items, you should be ready to fight:

- ENCHANTED SWORD
- ENCHANTED BOW (MUST HAVE INFINITY ENCHANTMENT)
- AN ARROW
- FULLY ENCHANTED NETHERITE ARMOUR
- POTION OF FEATHER FALLING
- SEVERAL HEALING SPLASH POTIONS
- AN IRON PICKAXE
- SEVERAL STACKS OF COBBLESTONE
- A STACK OF ENDER PEARLS

## WHAT TO LOOK OUT FOR

There will be a lot of Endermen on the ground beneath the dragon, so you'll need to dodge them while fighting. As long as you don't look in their eyes, you should be fine.

There are columns around the dragon, each of which has a crystal on top. These crystals will heal the dragon when she flies past. These must be destroyed as quickly as possible.

If you find yourself blasted into the air, your Feather Falling potions will help with landing. You could also throw an Ender pearl at the ground to reach safety quickly.

## TIME TO FIGHT!
The first thing to take care of is the crystals on the columns. You can shoot these with your bow but it will take some careful aiming. You'll need to aim much higher than the crystal to make up for the way the arrow arcs through the air. You could pillar up with cobblestone and smack it with your pickaxe, but it's possible to get hit by an explosion and thrown from the top.

Once these crystals are broken, the dragon won't be able to heal. She will begin flying around, occasionally coming to hover over the structure in the ground. The best action here is to try and hit her with arrows while she flies, and be prepared to rush in with your sword when she comes in to hover.

## DRAGON'S BREATH
This attack has a similar effect, but is blasted from her mouth in a 3 second burst. If you find yourself in the area of weakness, try to escape from the purple effect on the ground.

After several minutes of attacking the dragon and dodging her attacks, her health will run out and she will die in a spectacular burst of light. This small explosion creates a rain of XP orbs to fall from the sky for you to collect. Now you can hop into the open portal in the ground and leave her realm.

## The dragon has two main attacks:

### FIREBALL
These fireballs cannot be struck and reflected back at the dragon. They will hit the ground you're standing on and create an area of weakness to slowly damage you.

Congratulations, you beat the dragon and you finished the main goal of the game. Don't worry, after the credits roll, you'll find yourself back at home, ready to continue exploring, building and fighting.

# THE END

Once you've beaten the Ender dragon, you'll find that you have access to the End, a whole new dimension to explore which contains just as much treasure as there is danger. You've already had a glimpse of it while fighting the dragon, now it's time for adventure.

## HOW TO ENTER THE END

Once the dragon battle is over, begin looking around the island for a small gateway portal. The outer blocks are made of bedrock and there's a one block size portal, shimmering dark green and black.

You might be wondering how you get through the portal as it's much smaller than your character; the easiest way in, is to throw an Ender pearl through the gap. This will pull you through and into the End.

## TRAVELLING IN THE END

As you can see right away, the End is made of lots of floating islands. If you fall off the edge, the void will kill you and you'll spawn back to your bed. Moving through this dimension can be tricky. You'll need to either build lots of bridges using any blocks you have, or that are around you.

The other option, which is much more dangerous, is to throw Ender pearls in order to teleport across the gaps. Oh, and there are thousands of Endermen living here; angering just one will have several of them attempting to attack you.

## WHAT TO SEE AND DO

The main reason for coming to the End, is to find an elytra. This item is a pair of wings which allow you to fly when equipped. Elytra can only be found inside End ships, which are boats floating in the void.

Once you have found a ship, you'll need to get in and avoid danger from shulkers. The shulker mob is only found here, in the End. They're a bit like clams, with a shell that opens up for them to shoot you. If they manage to hit you, you'll find yourself floating in the air for several seconds with no control of your character.

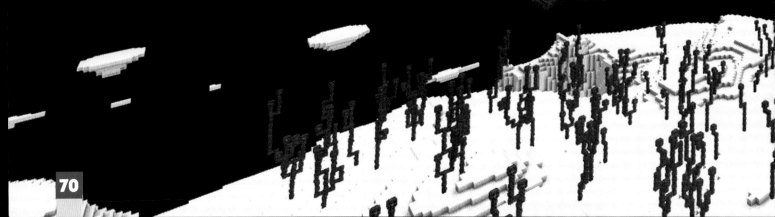

You can use your bow and, if you can get close enough, your sword too. You will want to kill as many shulkers as possible, you'll want what they drop - shulker shells.

Once you've found the elytra in the bottom of the ship, and collected a few shulker shells, it's time to head home. There are several exits in the End and you'll have to search around for them. They look the same as the entrance you came through and are scattered randomly throughout the islands. Thankfully they have beams shining from them, making them a little easier to find.

Those shulker shells you collected are very valuable. If you place them in a crafting table (as shown here) you'll create a shulker box. These are chests which you can fill up, then keep them in your inventory. This expands what you can carry because when you break the shulker box to pick it up, everything stays inside.

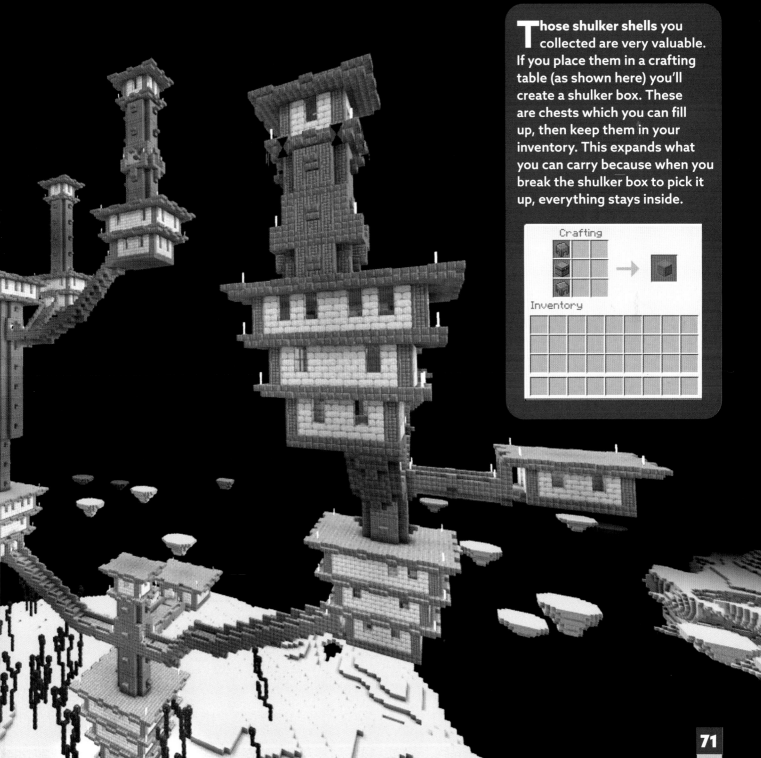

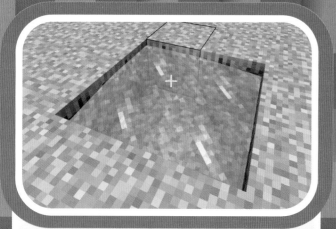

## INFINITE WATER

Setting up an infinite water source is super easy. Dig yourself a 2x2 hole and pour water into two opposite corners. This fills the hole and whenever you use your bucket, the water won't run out.

## INFINITE LAVA

You can also set up infinite lava sources, too. If you follow the image here, the lava will drip through the glass block, down the dripstone and into the cauldrons below.

# TIPS AND TRICKS

At any point in your Minecraft journey you will need lots of tips and tricks to make things a bit easier. Some things you learn over time, while others, we can let you in on and have you become a Minecraft master in no time.

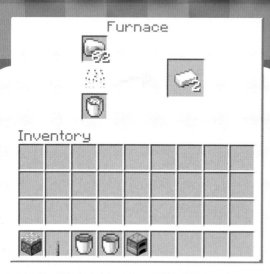

## NETHERITE UPGRADE

You don't need lots of netherite ingots to create armour, weapons and tools. All you need is a smithing table and one ingot per item. Place your diamond chestplate into the table along with one ingot and it transforms into a netherite chestplate.

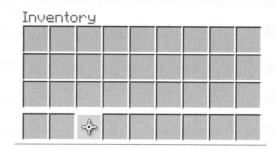

## FURNACE LAVA FUEL

You can always use coal or charcoal in your furnaces, but you can also use buckets of lava. This fuel will last a lot longer and can be filled infinitely which saves hunting for coal.

## FISHING DEPTHS
There are two levels to fishing. If you fish in shallow water, you'll only catch junk items along with salmon and cod. However, if you fish in the ocean, you can pull up enchanted bows or fishing rods, plus enchanted books.

## MUSIC DISCS
You can craft a jukebox to fill your home with some of the great Minecraft music, but you'll need music discs. These can be found in mineshafts and dungeons, but they also drop if a skeleton kills a creeper!

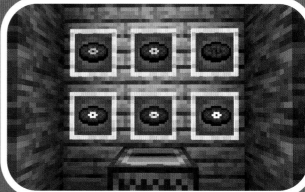

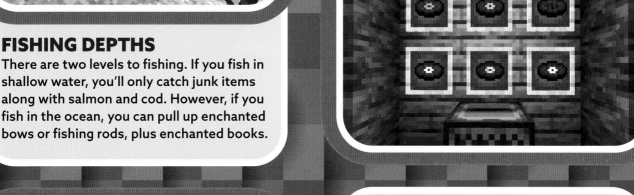

## NETHER SUNFLOWER
If you're desperately looking for a fortress in the Nether, you can use a sunflower from the Overworld to help out. Simply bring a block of dirt, place it and plant the flower. Whichever way the flower head points, is the direction of the fortress.

## BARREL AND FRAME STORAGE
Chests always need space above them to opened, even if that space is another chest. However, if there's a solid block above, they won't open. This isn't the case with barrels as they can be placed anywhere. Add some item frames and you can find what you need fast.

## WATER ELEVATOR
If you want to climb through deep holes in the ground quickly, a water elevator can help. Just pour the water in the top of the hole, at the bottom place some soul sand and when the hole is full, plant kelp all the way to the top. This creates water source blocks, while the soul sand shoots you upwards. Over 100 layers in just a few seconds!

# THE DEEP DARK

Created for one of the most recent updates, the deep dark is the scariest place to visit in the Overworld. As the name suggests, it's deep down in the layers of the world, and it's incredibly dark. However, it's what lives in the dark that is the most terrifying.

The deep dark is an Overworld biome that was added in the Caves and Cliffs update. There is no natural light in the cave system, making it difficult to find your way through. To add to this sense of danger, the deep dark is filled with sculk shriekers and sensors which, if disturbed by noise you make, can summon the Warden.

**ANCIENT CITY**

# THE WARDEN

The Warden is a very powerful mob who can easily kill your character if you aren't prepared. They have the most powerful attacks in Minecraft and can kill you in two hits. The Warden cannot see, they rely on the noise you make, and if they hear you they can send out a sonic boom attack that ignores your armour.

The Warden will wander around randomly, listening for sounds and the best way to deal with this is to sneak through the area, or place wool on the floor and walk on that instead. Wool makes no sound, so it's a great block to bring with you.

The Warden only appears if the player disturbs sculk shriekers four times. You will know if you have disturbed a shrieker by the noise it creates, and on the fourth time the Warden will rise out of the ground and begin to hunt you.

In some deep dark areas you might be lucky to find an ancient city. These abandoned cities spawn randomly and are beautiful, as well as fun to explore. Most of the pathways through will be made of wool or carpets because the ancient people that lived here were aware of the Warden.

If you look carefully and explore each and every corner, you might find a hidden door that leads to a long forgotten basement

There are always a couple of loot chests, but finding an ancient city is a builder's dream. The blocks and items here can be harvested and taken home to use in new builds. Keep a look out for soul lanterns, and remember, you can destroy and pick up the sculk blocks for a really unique building block.

# VILLAIN LAIR

**B**y now you've spent a lot of hours in Minecraft, exploring and building. You've been to the Nether and found lots of awesome materials. It's time to bring those home and build something extraordinary. Of course, if you're struggling to build in Survival Mode, feel free to switch to Creative Mode. Here we are building a villain lair in the side of a snowy mountain.

## TIP!

Try to think outside of the 'blocks' and use things like polished terracotta, which creates funky patterns.

## STEP ONE:

To start, we laid a wooden path up the side of a mountain and placed the foundations of an entry hallway.

After placing the doors, we added some details with fencing. All wood comes from the Nether crimson forest.

The walls are made from blackstone, and we used three versions of it, including gilded blackstone, which adds some nice details.

A couple of soul lanterns really add to the spooky feeling of this building.

## STEP TWO:

Rather than just using glass for the windows, why not add some metal railings to make everything feel menacing? We backed ours with some orange glass panes to highlight the lava we'll place down later.

Keep building up the walls with more blackstone. You can build rooms inside at this point if it's easier for you.

We added more railings to the top of the building. Behind this is a trench, 1 block deep, which we will fill with lava. Lava and fire makes everything look evil, mwhahahahaha!

## TIP!

If you're using creative, you'll have access to lots of items and objects that aren't in survival mode, like the heads of hostile mobs.

## STEP THREE:

Now we've added lava to the trench at the top, and behind fence columns at the side.

The columns are blackstone fences - without these fences the lava will spill out and begin to burn any wood in your build.

Finish rounding out the top of the building, and make sure your walls join up to the mountain behind.

You can shape the snow blocks to make the landscape feel more natural.

## STEP FOUR:

For the inside we've used more crimson fences to make a chandelier with more soul lanterns. This gives the building a nice medieval theme.

As do the suits of gold armour placed on stands next to the doors into the mountain.

Laying carpet really changes up the look of the building, but remember, you can't place items or blocks on top of carpet.

You can make this lair feel creepier with spiderwebs or mob heads in Creative, which will make all your visitors tremble in fear.